Crafts for Kids Who Are Wild About

Reptiles

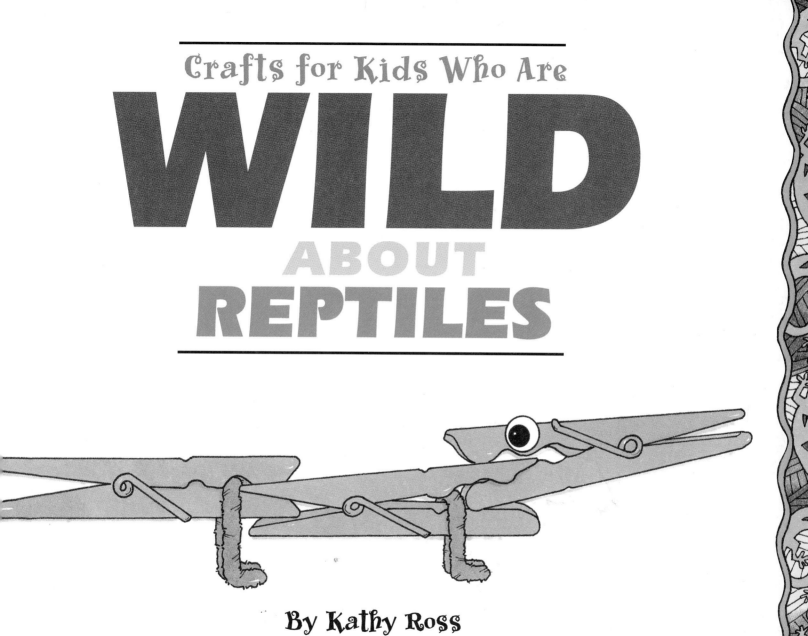

Crafts for Kids Who Are
WILD
ABOUT
REPTILES

By Kathy Ross
Illustrated by Sharon Lane Holm

The Millbrook Press   Brookfield, Connecticut

For my special friends Anne and Chris, even though one of them
may not be so wild about being in the same room with any of the
creatures in this book.—K.R.

To Lisa and Rick—S.L.H.

Library of Congress Cataloging-in-Publication Data
Ross, Kathy (Katharine Reynolds), 1948–
Crafts for kids who are wild about reptiles / Kathy Ross ; illustrated by Sharon Lane Holm.
p. cm.
Summary: Provides step-by-step instructions for using common household materials to make
model reptiles to be used as toys, for decoration, or for science projects.
ISBN 0-7613-0263-8 (lib. bdg.)   ISBN 0-7613-0332-4 (pbk.)
1. Handicraft—Juvenile literature.   2. Reptiles in art—Juvenile literature. [1. Reptiles in art.
2. Handicraft.] I. Holm, Sharon Lane, ill. II. Title.
TT160.R7142253   1998
745.59—dc21   97-27961   CIP   AC

Published by The Millbrook Press, Inc.
2 Old New Milford Road
Brookfield, Connecticut 06804

Contents

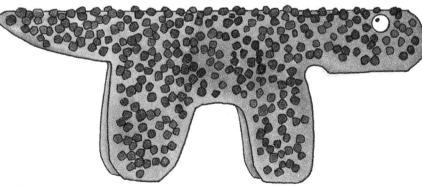

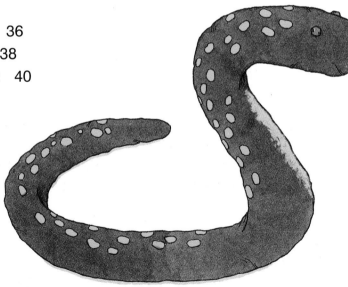

Introduction

I think that some of the strangest looking animals in the world are reptiles. There are four groups of reptiles left in the world today; turtles and tortoises, snakes and lizards, crocodilian, and, all by itself, the tuatara.

All reptiles are cold-blooded. This means that their body temperature is not constant but depends on the outside environment. Reptiles do not all look alike, but they all are covered with scales. Reptiles need air to breathe.

If you do not already have one or more books with colorful pictures of reptiles, I recommend that you go to the library and take some out. (I've suggested a few of the more interesting ones at the back of this book.) This will give you a clearer picture of what each animal actually looks like before you attempt to make it. The books will also give you lots of entertaining and interesting information about these amazing creatures.

Have a great time with the projects in this book. Join me in the fun of being "wild" about reptiles.

Kathy Ross

Paper Plate Chameleon

Here is what you need:

two paper plates
yellow pipe cleaner, 12 inches (30 cm) long
stapler
scissors
two cone-shaped party hats
two cloves
white glue
paintbrush and green and yellow poster paints
newspaper to work on
Styrofoam tray for drying

The tongue of the chameleon can be as much as twice as long as its body.

Here is what you do:

Fold one paper plate in half and staple it together at the top edge to hold the fold. This will be the body of the chameleon.

Fold the second plate in half and cut a pie-shaped wedge from it, with the fold, the cut, and the fluted edge of the plate all about 3½ inches (9 cm) long. This will be the head of the chameleon. Slide the folded piece partway over one end of the plate body and staple it in place so that the fold in the body forms an open mouth.

Cut four 5-inch (12.5-cm) legs from the fluted edge of the second paper plate. Staple a leg on each side of the front of the chameleon behind the head. Staple the other two legs toward the back of the chameleon one on each side.

Cut a long, curly tail from the center portion of the second paper plate. Staple the tail, curving down and under, between the folds at the back of the body.

Cut a 1-inch (2.5-cm) tip from the end of each party hat for the cone-shaped eyes of the chameleon. Glue one on each side of the head. (You can paint the tip of a cone-shaped paper cup instead.)

Paint the chameleon with green and yellow poster paint—or another color. Chameleons are known for their ability to change color to blend in with their surroundings. Decide where you are going to display your chameleon and paint it the same color as its background. Let the chameleon dry on the Styrofoam tray.

Dip the stems of two cloves into glue and then slip them onto the top of the eye cones. A real chameleon has eyes that can actually swivel around to look in different directions.

Dip the end of the yellow pipe cleaner in the glue, then slide it partway into the mouth. Leave most of the pipe cleaner sticking out for the amazingly long tongue.

You might want to make a small paper bug to glue on the tip of this hungry reptile's tongue.

Head of a Threatened Horned Toad

Here is what you need:

old adult-size brown sock
two tops with pull-up spouts from dish detergent
    bottles
red pipe cleaners
black permanent marker
scissors
masking tape
rubber band

The horned toad is actually a lizard, not a toad. When threatened, it will confuse and startle its enemies by squirting blood from its eyelids.

Here is what you do:

Cut the foot off the brown sock.
Cut a ½-inch (1¼ -cm) slit across
each side of the toe end of the sock.

Use the black permanent marker to
color the spouts of the two detergent
bottle tops. Tape the two spouts together,
side by side, to form the two eyes for the
horned toad. Slip the eyes inside the sock
foot and work one spout through each of the
cuts in the toe end of the sock. The black
spouts should now be sticking out of the
sock to look like two eyes.

Cut 2-inch (5-cm) spikes around the cuff of the top piece of sock. Slide the spiky sock over the foot piece so that the spikes at the head end stick out past the eyes. Hold the spiky sock in place around the eye caps with a rubber band. Fold the cut spikes back over the rubber band so that they stick out around the eyes to resemble the head of the spiky little horned toad.

Cut two 4-inch (10-cm) pieces of red pipe cleaner. Pull both eye spouts out to open them all the way. Slide one piece of red pipe cleaner down into each eye cap. Reach inside the sock puppet and pull each pipe cleaner down into the sock until the end is level with the opening in the spout. Dot the tip of the pipe cleaner with the black marker.

To use the puppet, just put your hand inside and push on the ends of the two pipe cleaners to make them come out of the eyes like squirting blood. The pipe cleaners weaken very quickly with use, so if your horned toad is easily threatened, it would be a good idea to have extra red pipe cleaners on hand for reloading.

Brown Anole Puppet

Here is what you need:

old adult-size brown sock
22-ounce plastic dish detergent bottle
cereal box cardboard
masking tape
two brown pipe cleaners, 12 inches (30 cm) long
small red balloon
scissors
sharp black marker

The reddish throat sack of the male anole lizard appears when the lizard is threatened or when it wishes to attract a female anole.

Here is what you do:

Cut an 8-inch (20-cm) tail for the lizard from the cardboard. Turn the plastic bottle on its side. Tape the tail to the side of the bottle so that it sticks out beyond the bottom of the bottle.

Pull the sock over the spout end of the bottle and down over the bottle and the tail, positioning the heel of the sock on the side of the bottle where the tail is taped. The toe stitching on the sock will form a mouth for the lizard at the spout end of the bottle.

Cut a 2-inch (5-cm) slit down from the mouth. Work the spout of the bottle out through the slit. Open the spout. Pull the neck of the red balloon down over the spout. Pull the end of the sock back over the spout and balloon.

 Poke one pipe cleaner into the front, bottom side of the sock covering of the lizard. Pass it underneath the bottle, then out through the other side of the sock so that the two ends of the pipe cleaners form the lizard's two front legs. Bend the ends of the pipe cleaner into little feet. Use the other pipe cleaner to make back legs in the same way.

Draw two eyes for the lizard on masking tape. Cut out each eye and stick it in place above the mouth of the lizard.

To use the puppet, just squeeze the bottle to inflate the red balloon. It will resemble the exposed throat sac of the male anole.

Gila Monster Finger Puppet

Here is what you need:

cardboard toilet-tissue tube
old glove
peppercorns
two tiny wiggle eyes
paintbrush and black poster paint
pink nail polish
white glue
plastic margarine tub for mixing glue and paint
pencil
scissors
newspaper to work on
Styrofoam tray for drying

The shy and poisonous Gila monster is often called the beaded lizard because of its pink and black beaded covering.

Here is what you do:

Turn the cardboard tube on its side. Use the pencil to sketch the head, body, and tail of the Gila monster lengthwise along the tube. Sketch the legs coming down and around from the body on the curved sides of the tube. Cut the lizard out.

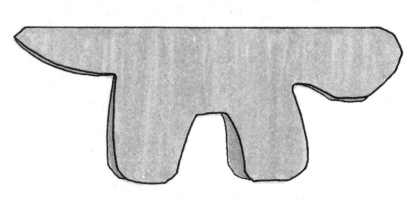

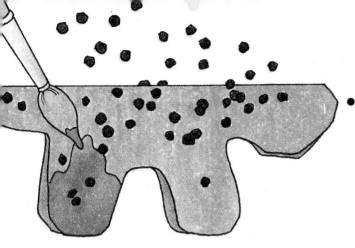

 Mix one part glue to two parts black paint. Paint both sides of the lizard. Immediately sprinkle peppercorns all over the wet top and legs of the lizard to make the beaded skin. Make sure that the entire lizard is covered. Let the glue and paint dry.

Use the pink nail polish to make areas of pink beads on the lizard.

Cut a finger from the glove. Glue the finger underneath the lizard with the opening at the back.

Glue two wiggle eyes on the head.

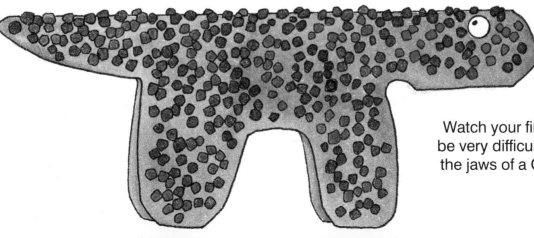

Watch your fingers! It can be very difficult to pry open the jaws of a Gila monster.

Flying Dragon Glider

Here is what you need:

brown pipe cleaner, 12 inches (30 cm) long
brown construction paper
sheet of white paper
paper basket-type coffee filter
white glue
cellophane tape
masking tape
plastic drinking straw
scissors
container to mix glue and paint
brown poster paint
paintbrush
sharp black marker
newspaper to work on
Styrofoam tray for drying

Flaps of skin over elongated ribs allow the flying dragon to glide from branch to branch.

Here is what you do:

Draw the outline of a head, body, and tail on the brown paper. Make the lizard about 12 inches (30 cm) long overall. Cut out the lizard.

Flatten the coffee filter and fold it in half. Glue the body in the center of the folded filter with the head sticking out at the flat side. The filter should now stick out on both sides to form the "wings" of the lizard.

Mix one part glue to t[] parts brown paint. Pa[] lizard on both sides with the paint mixture. Let the project flat on a Styrofoam tray. The [] in the paint will stiffen the filte[] "wings" to give them t[] strength needed to glide.

Cut the pipe cleaner in half. Glue one piece across the bottom front portion of the lizard to form the front legs. Secure the glued legs with masking tape. Glue the second piece of pipe cleaner across the bottom, back portion of the lizard in the same way. Wait until the glue has dried, then shape the legs and bend the ends to form feet.

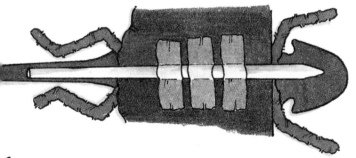

Cut a strip of white paper about 9 inches (23 cm) long and 1½ inches (4 cm) wide. Roll the strip around the straw. Use cellophane tape to hold the paper in the rolled position. The paper should slide on and off the straw easily. Fold the top open end of the paper into a triangle shape. Use tape to seal off the opening. Tape the rolled paper to the bottom of the lizard with the sealed end at the head.

To use the puppet, just blow on the straw and watch your flying dragon glide through the air.

Licking Gecko

Here is what you need:

green construction paper
pencil
bubble wrap with small bubbles
two flat buttons
masking tape
old red or pink glove
white glue
stapler
scissors

The gecko has no eyelids, so it must use its long tongue to keep its eyes moist.

Here is what you do:

Draw the outline of the top view of the gecko on the green paper. Cut out the outline.

Staple a piece of bubble wrap, flat side down, over the lizard. Trim the bubble wrap to fit, then add more staples around the outside of the lizard to hold it in place.

Glue the two buttons to the head of the lizard for eyes. Put a piece of masking tape on the bubble wrap where you want to glue each eye. This will create an area the glue will stick to.

Cut a finger from the glove to make a tongue for the puppet. Use masking tape to tape the open end of the tongue under one side of the head. You should place the tongue so that when you slip your finger in it, you can curl it up to lick the eyes of the gecko. When you have the tongue properly placed, use the stapler to secure it.

Geckos come in a variety of colors and patterns. You might want to make your gecko a different color.

Bag Komodo Dragon

Here is what you need:

five large brown paper grocery bags
paper-towel tube
paintbrush and white, pink, and black poster paint
bubble wrap with small bubbles
masking tape
white glue
newspaper for stuffing and to work on
black marker
crinkle-cut scissors

The biggest lizard in the world is the Komodo dragon.

Here is what you do:

Open two bags and stuff them almost to the top with crumpled newspaper. Slide the opening of one bag over the opening of the other and glue them together. This will be the body of the Komodo dragon.

To make the head, use crinkle-cut scissors to cut the bottom out of a bag. Cut a triangle-shaped piece out of each side of the bag so that the opening looks like a mouth with sharp teeth. Slide the top of the bag over one end of the body and glue it in place.

Cut the paper-towel tube in half and use one half to make a tongue. Cut a fork in one end of the tongue. Glue the other end in the bottom back of the mouth between the two bags.

Slide the opening of an empty bag over the back of the body and glue it in place.

Flatten out the last bag. Fold the bottom of the bag into a point and glue it in place. Use masking tape to help hold the folds. This will be the tip of the tail. Glue the opening of the tail to the bottom of the last bag. The folded part of the tail should be facing down so that the top is smooth.

To give the lizard a scaly look, print the entire body using bubble wrap: Paint over a piece of wrap with black paint and print the bubble shapes on the lizard. Keep repainting the bubbles until you have printed the entire body.

Paint the inside of the mouth pale pink. Give the tongue a thick coating of white paint. Use the black marker to draw eyes on the top of the head and crouching legs on each side of the body.

Real Komodo dragons can be up to 10 feet (3 m) long. If you want your dragon to be longer, just add more stuffed bags to its middle.

Foil and Tissue Glass Snake

Here is what you need:

aluminum foil
black tissue paper or white tissue paper
paintbrush and black, green, and white poster paint
white glue
scissors
two peppercorns
plastic margarine tub for mixing
Styrofoam trays for drying
newspaper to work on

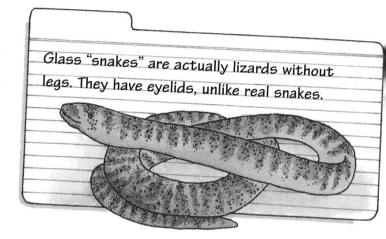

Glass "snakes" are actually lizards without legs. They have eyelids, unlike real snakes.

Here is what you do:

Tear off a strip of aluminum foil 18 inches (46 cm) long, or more if you want your snake to be longer. Squeeze the sides of the foil together to make a long foil tube for the body of the snake. If the snake seems too thin, squeeze another layer of foil around the first layer. Round off the foil at one end for a head. Squeeze the foil into a point at the other end for the tail.

Cut a long piece of tissue paper to fit around the snake. If your snake is very long, you may need more than one piece. Shape the foil into the position you want your snake to be.

 If the snake is not already black, paint it black. Paint the underside a whitish color. Mix some white and green paint on a Styrofoam tray and dab tiny light green spots all over the back of the snake.

Glue two peppercorns to the head of the snake for eyes.

Mix one part water to two parts glue in the margarine tub. Paint the entire snake with the watery glue. Working on a Styrofoam tray on newspapers, cover the snake with tissue paper. Paint the outside of the snake with more watery glue, being careful not to damage the tissue paper. If you do tear the tissue, it is easily patched with more tissue, but try to keep the tissue skin as smooth as possible, just like a real glass snake. Let the project dry hard across a Styrofoam tray.

This glass snake dries so stiff that it can't move at all!

Shedding Snake

Here is what you need:

a long white sock, such as a woman's knee sock
red pipe cleaner, 12 inches (30 cm) long
black permanent marker
white glue
scissors
paintbrush and green poster paint
fiberfill
rubber band
old pair of pantyhose
newspaper to work on
Styrofoam tray for drying

A snake will outgrow and shed its skin many times during its lifetime.

Here is what you do:

To make the snake, stuff the entire sock with fiberfill. Close the open end of the sock with a rubber band. This will be the tail end of the snake.

Paint the entire snake with green paint.

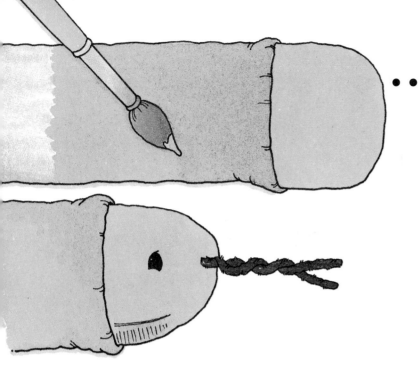

Cut off one leg of the pantyhose. Starting at the tail of the snake, pull the stocking leg over the entire snake for the skin. Paint the stocking green while it is over the snake, and let it dry.

Fold the red pipe cleaner in half and twist it together with the ends spread slightly apart to make the forked tongue. Cut a tiny hole in the toe end of the sock. Dip the folded end of the pipe cleaner in glue and stick it in the hole so that the tongue is sticking out of the head.

Use the marker to draw eyes on the head of the snake. You can draw eyes on the skin over the head, too.

To shed its skin, a snake will rub its head against something rough and continue rubbing until it slips totally out of the old skin. Try this with your snake.

Cobra About to Strike

Here is what you need:

necktie in muted colors
red paper scrap
aluminum foil
two pèppercorns
masking tape
white glue
scissors
newspaper to work on

The cobra curls its body, lifts its head, and spreads its hood when preparing to strike.

Here is what you do:

Tear off long pieces of aluminum foil and squeeze them into long strips. Squeeze the ends of the foil strips together until you have a single band the length of the necktie. Thread the foil band through the length of the tie.

The wide end of the tie will be the hooded head of the cobra. Wrap masking tape around the portion of the foil band that is exposed.

Cut a forked tongue for the snake from the red paper. Glue the tape-wrapped foil to the underside of the tie with the tongue between the point of the tie and the taped foil.

4 Glue two peppercorns at the pointed end of the tie above the tongue for eyes.

The foil inside the tie will allow you to shape the snake into a striking position with the body curled and the head lifted up. Pretty scary!

Bags Python

Here is what you need:

several paper lunch bags
red ribbon
two bubbles cut from bubble wrap with large bubbles
plastic berry basket
two peppercorns
newspaper for stuffing and to work on
white glue
scissors
masking tape
paintbrush and green and yellow poster paint
Styrofoam trays for drying

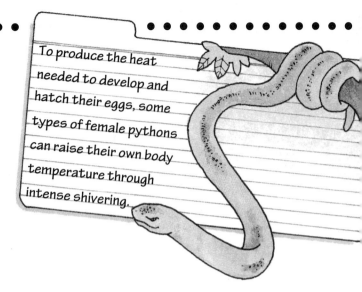

To produce the heat needed to develop and hatch their eggs, some types of female pythons can raise their own body temperature through intense shivering.

Here is what you do:

Open one lunch bag and stuff it to the top with crumpled newspaper. Do the same with the second lunch bag. Rub glue around the edge of the open end of the second bag and glue it over the open rim of the first bag.

Stuff a third bag. Rub glue around the bottom edge of one of the attached bags and glue the open end of the third bag to it. Continue adding stuffed bags until the snake is as long as you want it to be.

Fold the bottom of a lunch bag into a point. Glue the folds in place and use masking tape to hold the fold. Slip the open end of this bag over the line of stuffed bags to form the tail of the snake. Glue in place.

Paint the bag snake green and let it dry. Paint the bottom of a berry basket with yellow paint. Use the wet basket bottom to print scales over the entire green body of the snake, repainting the basket as necessary to print the entire snake.

Cut a tiny slit in the back of each large-bubble-wrap bubble. Slip a peppercorn eyeball into each and glue the bubble eyes to the head end of the snake.

Cut a piece of red ribbon 9 inches (23 cm) long. Cut a fork in one end of the ribbon. Glue the other end under the front bag of the snake to look like a tongue sticking out of its mouth.

Pythons are the longest snakes in the world. How long is your python?

Annoyed Rattlesnake Rattle

Here is what you need:

cardboard wrapping-paper tube, 1 inch (2.5 cm) in
    diameter
pair of pantyhose
black pipe cleaner, 12 inches (5 cm) long
paintbrush and black, white, and brown poster paint
plastic film canister with lid
rice
newspaper to work on
Styrofoam trays for drying

Here is what you do:

Put some rice in the film canister and snap the lid on. This will be the rattle for the snake.

You can always tell when a rattlesnake is annoyed because you can hear it rattling its tail.

Cut both legs off the pantyhose. Slide one leg over the length of the cardboard tube. Pull the stocking tight over the tube and knot the open end to hold it in place. Put the rattle in the excess stocking at the knotted end and knot the open end of the stocking again to hold the rattle in place. Make the rattle sit at a slight angle to the end of the tube.

Slide the second stocking over the tube, starting at the end with the rattle. Pull it tight over the tube snake and knot the opening closed at the other end, placing a folded black pipe cleaner in the knot. Twist the two ends of the pipe cleaner together, then spread the two ends slightly to make a forked tongue for the snake. Trim the extra stocking from the knot, then slide the knot to the underside of the snake.

Paint the snake brown, then dab black and white paint over the body. Paint two black eyes at the head end.

Shake the snake to hear it rattle.

Designer Snake

Here is what you need:

fifteen or more empty thread spools of the same size
masking tape
three or more red pipe cleaners
white glue
paintbrush and poster paints
two sequins
lots of different ribbons and trims
Styrofoam trays for drying
newspaper to work on

There are about 2,500 different species of snakes in the world. Make your own favorite or design a new one

Here is what you do:

1 If the spools are plastic instead of wood, you will need to wrap them with masking tape to create a surface the paint and glue will stick to.

2 Bend the ends of two pipe cleaners together to make one long pipe cleaner strip. If you want a snake longer than this, just add one or more pipe cleaners. String a spool to the end of the pipe cleaner strip. Bend the end of the pipe cleaner over the end of the spool and use masking tape to hold it in place.

Continue to thread spools on the pipe cleaner strip until the snake is the length you wish it to be. Leave about 2 inches (5 cm) of pipe cleaner sticking out the end of the last spool. Slide another piece of pipe cleaner in the spool hole next to it and twist the two together with the ends slightly spread to make a forked tongue.

Decorate spool sections of the snake by using paints, trims, or both. You could make your snake look like a real snake or design a wild one of your own.

Paint over the masking tape at the head of the snake and over the masking tape at the end of the snake. Glue two sequins to the head above the tongue for eyes.

Does your snake have the coloring of a real snake, or is it definitely an original design?

Hissing Tuatara

Here is what you need:

empty soda can, washed and dried completely
a tablespoon of sand
aluminum foil
masking tape
two cats'-eye marbles
brown tissue paper
white glue
plastic margarine tub for mixing
Styrofoam tray for drying
newspaper to work on

The tuatara is the only living member of its order of reptiles, the rest of which died out millions of years ago. That is why the tuatara is called a "living fossil."

Here is what you do:

Put about a tablespoon of sand into the soda can. Seal the opening of the can with masking tape.

Tear off a piece of aluminum foil 2 feet (61 cm) long. Wrap the foil around the can with about 4 inches (10 cm) of the foil sticking out from the top of the can to shape into a head. Squeeze the excess foil sticking out from the bottom of the can into a band that comes to a point for the tail of the tuatara.

Tear off another piece of foil about 6 inches (15 cm) long. Squeeze the foil into a strip for the front legs and feet of the tuatara. Shape five clawed toes at the end of each foot. Repeat to make the back legs.

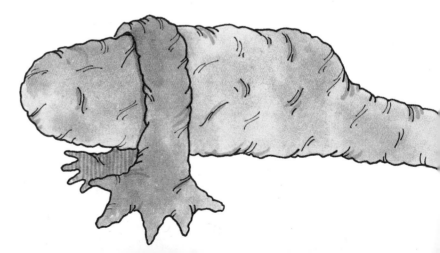

Bend the two sets of legs over the back of the tuatara so that there are front and back feet on each side. Use masking tape to hold the leg strips in place.

Pinch a crest up from the foil on the back of the tuatara, starting behind the head and running down the back to the end of the tail.

Mix two parts glue with one part water in a margarine tub. Dip pieces of brown tissue into the watery glue and use them to cover the entire tuatara. Push the foil claws through the tissue to make them stand out.

Use your fingers to push an eye socket into the foil on each side of the head. Glue a small piece of masking tape into each socket and onto each marble to create better gluing surfaces. Glue a marble in each hole for eyes.

When the glue has dried, shake your tuatara and listen to it hiss.

Ornate Box Turtle Wall Hanging

Here is what you need:

9-inch (23-cm) paper plate
three cardboard egg cartons
cereal box cardboard
black marker
white glue
twenty pieces of elbow macaroni
paintbrush and green, brown, and yellow poster paint
scissors
two small dried peas or lentils
hole punch
yellow yarn
newspaper to work on
Styrofoam tray for drying

The hinged bottom shell of the ornate box turtle can close completely to protect the turtle when it senses danger.

Here is what you do:

Trace around the paper plate on the cardboard for the bottom shell of the turtle. Draw a head, legs, and a tail on the sides of the shell. Cut the turtle shape out.

From the bottoms of about 25 egg cups, cut pieces that are ½ inch (1.25 cm) high. You will need enough to cover the entire shell of the turtle.

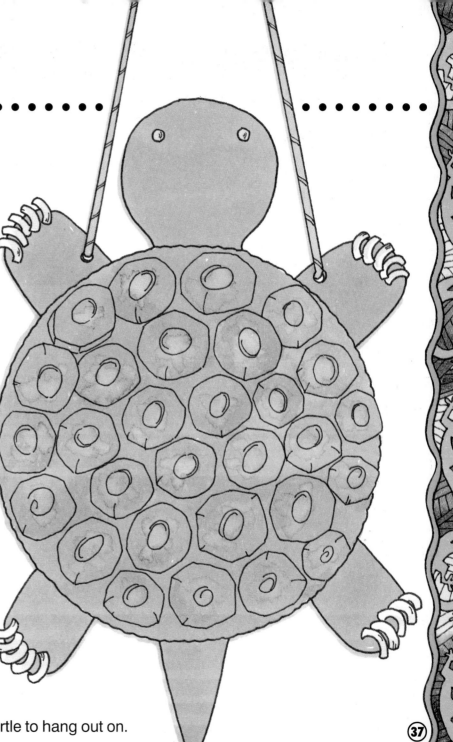

 Glue the paper plate, eating side down, over the shell portion of the turtle outline to form the top shell. Cover the shell with a thick layer of glue, then cover the glue with the egg cups, glued bottom side up. Let the glue dry.

Paint the entire top of the turtle green or brown with dabs of yellow on the shell portion.

Glue five macaroni claws on each foot. Glue two dried peas or lentils on the head for eyes.

Punch a hole on the side of each front leg toward the head. Cut a piece of yellow yarn 2 feet (61 cm) long. String one end of the yarn through the back of each hole and tie the ends together to make a hanger.

Find a wall or door for your turtle to hang out on.

In and Out Red-eared Terrapin

Here is what you need:

small paper bowl
cereal box cardboard
four wooden ice-cream spoons
two craft sticks
small sliding matchbox
masking tape
scissors
stapler
a few strands of dry spaghetti
black marker
paintbrush and brown, yellow, and red poster paint
white glue
newspaper to work on
Styrofoam tray for drying

Here is what you do:

Trace around the rim of the bowl on the cardboard. Cut out the circle. The upside-down bowl will be the top shell of the turtle, and the cardboard circle will be the bottom shell.

Glue the four wooden spoons to the print side of the cardboard circle so that they stick out for the legs of the turtle. Glue the craft stick on the edge of the circle so that it sticks out for the tail. Use masking tape to help secure the glued sticks.

The red-eared terrapin is easy to recognize. It has a red stripe along each side of its head.

Staple the upside-down bowl over the cardboard circle so that the legs and tail stick out from the sides.

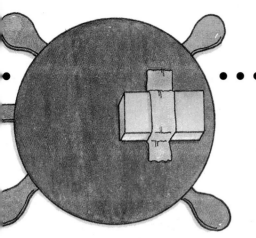

Paint the entire turtle brown, then dab some yellow on the shell. Slide the inner box out of the matchbox and paint the short sides and bottom brown with dabs of yellow. Paint the two long sides red for the band of color on each side of the terrapin's head. Let the project dry.

Glue the outer box of the matchbox on the bottom edge of the turtle where the head should come out. Use masking tape to hold it in place while the glue dries.

Cut a slit along the bottom of one of the short sides of the inner box. Slide the end of a craft stick into the slit and glue it to the bottom of the box. Use masking tape to hold it in place.

Slide the inner box, stick first, into the outer box under the shell so that the stick is hidden under the turtle. By pushing and pulling on the stick, you can make the turtle's head go in and out. Use a black marker to draw eyes on the turtle head.

Break off tiny pieces of spaghetti and glue five to the end of each leg forclaws.

This red-eared terrapin can move its head in and out of its shell just like a real one can.

Alligator Snapping Turtle Puppet

Here is what you need:

four 9-inch (23-cm) paper plates
two long white socks
elbow macaroni
two flat black buttons
stapler
white glue
scissors
old tennis ball
piece of pink or red pipe cleaner
paintbrush and brown, white, and red poster paint
old glove
two small wiggle eyes
newspaper to work on

The alligator snapping turtle has a wormlike appendage in the bottom of its mouth to lure its dinner, right between its powerful jaws.

Here is what you do:

Ask an adult to cut a slit across an old tennis ball using a sharp knife. Put the ball, cut end first, down in the toe of one of the socks. This will be the head of the alligator turtle. Push the end of the sock into the slit in the tennis ball to form a mouth for the turtle.

Cut the cuff end of the long sock that the head is in into a point to form the tail of the turtle.

Cut the foot off the second sock. Flatten the foot portion so that the bottom of the sock is underneath. Cut the foot into four equal pieces for the legs of the turtle.

4 Arrange the legs on the rim of the eating side of a paper plate. Set another plate, eating side up, on top of the first plate and staple the plates together at the legs to hold them in place. This will be the bottom shell of the turtle.

5 Staple two more plates together to make the top shell. Staple the plates, bottom side up, on each side of the bottom shell so that you can fit your hand and arm in between the top and bottom shells.

6 Paint the top and bottom shells and the legs brown. Paint the head and the tail of the turtle brown. Paint the inside of the turtle's mouth a reddish pink color. Use the white paint to lighten the red paint a little.

7 Glue five macaroni claws on the end of each leg.

Poke a piece of pipe cleaner into the bottom of the turtle's mouth to make the wormlike appendage. Glue the buttons above the mouth to make eyes. Slide the head between the top and bottom shells so that the head sticks out one end and the tail out the other end.

Make a tiny fish for the turtle to catch by cutting a finger from an old glove and gluing two wiggle eyes on the tip.

To use your alligator snapping turtle, place your hand into the head sock and put your fingers on each side of the cut tennis ball. By squeezing the ball on each side, the mouth of the turtle will open and the appendage will wiggle. Put the fish on a finger of your other hand, and show how the turtle catches dinner.

Tiny Turtle Necklace

Here is what you need:

- three cotton swabs
- two tiny wiggle eyes
- green plastic bottle cap
- white glue
- paintbrush and green and black poster paint
- yellow yarn
- scissors
- Styrofoam tray to work on

Here is what you do:

1. Cut a 1-inch (2.5-cm) piece off both ends of all three cotton swabs.

2. Paint the pieces green, with a dab of black paint on the tip of each one.

3. Turn the bottle cap upside down and fill it with glue. Arrange the stick ends of the swabs around the inside of the glue-filled lid so that the cotton ends stick out around the lid to form the four legs, the head, and the tail of the turtle.

4. Cut a piece of yarn 2 feet (61 cm) long for a hanger for the necklace. Put the two ends of the yarn in the glue on each side of the turtle head. Let the glue dry completely. This could take two or three days.

5. Turn the turtle over and glue two tiny wiggle eyes to the head.

Reptiles with shells are called chelonians. You probably know them as turtles and tortoises.

When the glue has dried, this chelonian will be ready to wear. Of course, most people will just want to call it a turtle.

Mother Crocodile

Here is what you need:

long cardboard gift-wrap tube about 1½ inches
    (4 cm) across
cardboard paper-towel tube
cereal box cardboard
two cotton balls
masking tape
dark color paper scrap
white glue
scissors
crinkle-cut scissors
paintbrush and red, white, brown, and green poster
    paint
newspaper to work on

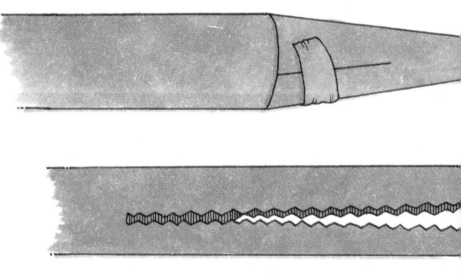

While the crocodile is a dangerous and easily angered animal, it is a remarkably good mother to its young.

Here is what you do:

Cut a slit halfway up the paper-towel tube. Wrap the cut end of the tube around itself to form a pointed tail. Hold the wrapped tube in place with masking tape. Glue the uncut end of the tube into one end of the longer tube, which will form the crocodile's body and head. Use crinkle-cut scissors to cut a mouth for the crocodile from the head end of the wrapping-paper tube. Cut a jagged slit about 8 inches (20 cm) long out of each side to look like an open mouth full of teeth.

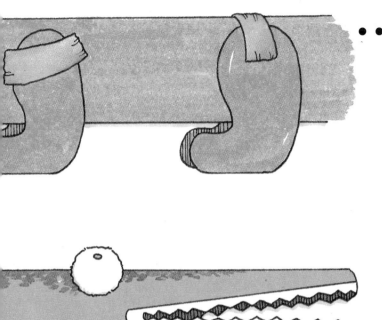

 Cut four legs from the cardboard. Glue two on each side of the body portion of the crocodile. Use masking tape to help hold them in place.

 If you wish to make your crocodile look scaly, you can cover the body with torn pieces of masking tape.

Paint the inside of the mouth red, the teeth white, and the rest of the crocodile a green and brown color.

Glue two cotton balls above the cut jaws of the crocodile for eyes. Cut pupils from scrap paper and glue them in place.

You might want to color and cut out some baby crocodiles to ride around in your mother crocodile's mouth.

Clothespin Alligator

Here is what you need:

three spring-type wooden clothespins
pipe cleaner, 6 inches (15 cm) long
two large wiggle eyes
paintbrush and yellow and green poster paint
white glue
scissors
newspaper to work on

The sex of the baby alligator is influenced by the temperature of the nest. This is called TSD (temperature-dependent sex determination).

Here is what you do:

Hold one clothespin open. Pinch a second clothespin over the top of the open clothespin and glue it in place. This will be the head of the alligator, and the first clothespin will be the body.

To make the tail, attach the third clothespin to the back top of the first clothespin and glue it in place.

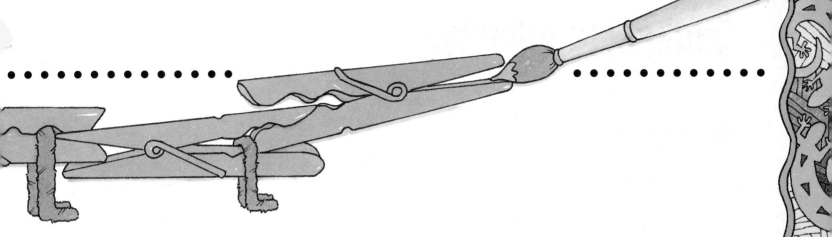

 Cut the pipe cleaner into two pieces. Slide one piece through the body clothespin toward the front to form front legs on each side. Bend the legs down and bend the ends forward to shape feet. Slide the second piece of pipe cleaner between the top end of the body clothespin and the tail or back legs. Shape legs and feet as you did with the front legs.

Paint the inside of the alligator's mouth pale yellow. Paint the rest of the alligator, including the legs, green.

Glue a wiggle eye to each side of the alligator's head.

Don't worry about the open mouth. That is how an alligator cools off.

Books About Reptiles

● ●

Bender, Lionel. *Fish to Reptiles*. New York: Gloucester Press, 1988.

Caitlin, Stephen. *Discovering Reptiles and Amphibians*. Mahwah, NJ: Troll Associates, 1990.

Chatfield, June. *A Look Inside Reptiles.* Pleasantville, NY: Reader's Digest Young Families, 1995.

Chermayeff, Ivan. *Scaly Facts.* San Diego, CA: Harcourt Brace, 1995.

Creagh, Carson. *Reptiles.* Alexandria, VA: Time-Life Books, 1996.

Elliott, Leslee. *Really Radical Reptiles and Amphibians.* New York, NY: Sterling, 1994.

Heller, Ruth. *Ruth Heller's How to Hide a Crocodile & Other Reptiles.* New York: Grosset & Dunlap, 1994.

Ling, Mary. *Amazing Crocodiles and Reptiles.* New York: Knopf, 1991.

Llamas Ruiz, Andres. *Reptiles and Amphibians: Birth and Growth.* New York: Sterling, 1996.

Parker, Steve. *Revolting Reptiles.* Austin, TX: Raintree Steck-Vaughn, 1994.

Retan, Walter. *101 Wacky Facts About Snakes & Reptiles.* New York, NY: Scholastic, 1991.

Ricciuti, Edward R. *Reptiles.* Woodbridge, CT: Blackbirch Press, 1993.

Richardson, Joy. *Reptiles.* New York: Franklin Watts, 1993.

Roberts, M. L. *World's Weirdest Reptiles.* Mahwah, NJ: Watermill Press, 1994.

Spinelli, Eileen. *Reptiles*. Lincolnwood, IL: Publications International, Ltd., 1991.

Stonehouse, Bernard. *A Closer Look at Reptiles.* New York: Gloucester Press, 1979.

Tesar, Jenny E. *What on Earth Is a Tuatara?* Woodbridge, CT: Blackbirch Press, 1994.

Wise, William. *Giant Snakes and Other Amazing Reptiles.* New York: Putnam, 1970.